Lovers in Theory

N.M.Sanchez

Cover photo by Karel Chladek
Co-Editor, Benjamin F.

ISBN-13: 9781983819605

For lovers that once were,
are, will be — or have always been.

CONTENTS

I.

History of Love

N.M.SANCHEZ

I am composed of many women — extensions of myself.
Women who carry histories
that wished for happier endings.

Women who loved and were loved in return,
but whose stories were reduced to drafts.

When memory visits, she gifts me a box:
revealing photographs, letters, and ticket stubs,
witness to a life with somebody else.

Split-soul theory postulates that two souls

could truly be one in the same

but faced separation,

destined to spend their lives attempting to reconnect.

How often have we found each other,

only to be condemned to lose each other eventually?

For how long have we been cursed to an endless cycle

of lost and found — then lost, again?

How does one measure either of the two?

Knowing you my entire life
and feeling as if it were but a moment

or knowing you for a moment
and feeling as though it has been my entire life?

Grateful for the way

my love holds you

throughout times

when I physically cannot.

Like the Hollywood divine, I fear tragedy will strike us

the way it does to most good people,

the way it does to those who don't deserve it

but had something coming, anyway.

I'll give you all I have while we still can,

while I'm still in charge of the script

and this direction:

roll the tape.

Bodies pressed together, open-mouthed and breathless.

My hands, desperate to grab onto anything before the bloom.

Our meeting was more than merely a product of luck,

we were written by the gods.

All that is in me aches to touch you,

all that is in you is fleeting:

I won't ask a lover to stay.

I've spent nights crying pain into poetry.

He tells you that he's leaving.
This is abrupt.

The last few weeks play back in your mind
like a feature film
and you analyze previous conversations.

Was it — could it be — is it her?
The answer is yes.

A brittle spine, unsteady legs,
clenched fists.

Your latest version of love
is torn from your hands,
becomes somebody else's.

To build a home throughout the years

that comes crashing down in seconds — irreparable,

nearly unrecognizable and nothing left to salvage.

Sometimes, the end is inevitable.

Sometimes, there's nothing left to do but cry.

When you ache,

I come running.

When I ache,

you leave me that way.

We are with others while thinking of each other.

What does that make us?

What does that say about us,

other than being fleeting cowards in nature

and lovers in thought?

LOVERS IN THEORY

He bites down into my thigh like fresh fruit,

an attempt to satiate the hunger.

Each time, "the last time"

because no one knows

because no one has had to know

because we do not exist outside of the bedroom.

When he says, "I am incapable of leading two lives"

what he means to say is that he's not choosing me.

And I know this, but I bite the bullet — claim my foolishness

and take what he is willing to give me.

Different lives that call for different responsibilities,

people and events to attend to without the other.

In this world, the only place we are allowed to exist in

is in secret.

And like any secret held for far too long,

it grows hands and teeth and a heartbeat,

a steady grip that claws into me,

like any dying thing that begs for mercy.

Drank about you last night,

hungover you this morning.

LOVERS IN THEORY

I'm not allowed to love you,

but since when has that stopped

the emergence of a feeling?

One false move is a slip onto the land mine,

     [explosion]

an innocent caught in the crossfire.

But you look my way and it's over.

     [scattered pieces]

I have tried to keep my distance out of fear

I would wake the dream from its slumber,

that the dream would taste the life it knows

it would have to live without you.

But my heart is no stranger to the shape of you

and hell, I'm already grieving.

I merely needed to know

if the years we spent

unraveling each other

was out of love.

You still think of me between months, years of my absence.

You find reflections of my character in others,

cued to remember me when you find yourself

near the places we used to visit.

Is that not intimacy?

Is that not the dreamer within you aching for another reality

in which we are allowed to exist in — together?

What else is that emotional pull

but the soul reaching for hands that dream of it, too?

I told myself to kiss you,

to breathe in the bravery

and exhale the fear

before the memory is molded into history

and I recall this night

as the night *I should have kissed you.*

Going once, going twice:

I pucker my lips

and shut my eyes,

this is how I want you to remember me.

We romanticize romantic relationships so often
we forget there are other forms of intimacy to experience:

A subtle look across the room
that transmits a mutual thought,

a smirk that forms at the corner of your mouth,

the grazing of hands — the holding,
the hand on the shoulder,

a kiss on the cheek,
a letter,
a gesture,

the various acts of kindness
between friends, family, and strangers.

It was fruitless and repetitive:

how often I would offer my body
thinking he'd come to love me, eventually.

I have burned for a man,
caught fire in the waiting.

How often I have slept with masochism
instead of running.

How often I have hung on,
bruised by love's defeat,
expecting a different outcome.

There is an ache when I think of you:

something beautiful,
something missing,
something we started
but left unfinished.

Yet what is written is fiery.

A feeling that lingers,
a love not fully explored,
untouched, salivating,
and yet — bruised.

LOVERS IN THEORY

Love does not understand why you don't want it back,
why you won't call, or ask how it's been doing.
Love does nothing but cry in-between lunch breaks
or during songs that elicit memories.

Love does not know how to blame you,
how to become angry at the thought
that you cannot simply text back.
Love blames itself,
love formulates excuses for your fuck-ups.

Love is irrational, unable to comprehend
where it isn't welcomed, where it is no longer wanted,
where it no longer needs to be.

Love,
desperately and in all its glory,
will sit and wait with all its wanting — foolishly hoping
you return with a kiss.

I wonder how often the world

reminds you of me,

because it won't let me forget you.

I offer myself to you as if I were handing over
the scarcity of water in the middle of the desert.

Cautiously, but lending faith in your ability to ration,
to handle with care — to give some of it back.

Do you recognize this kind of sacrifice?

The way we give ourselves to the fire
to learn if we can survive it?

I don't know what to do with myself, you know?

I'm reckless — hopelessly invested

and looking for any subtle hint suggesting

you still think of me.

You sit perfectly still, perched up, on the edge,
attentive to the stories he tells:

and everything is of interest.

You notice his hands,
dense and full of past accounts, of turmoil.

And you wonder how many times
he has had to pull himself out from the wreckage.

You notice the way his left eyebrow raises
slightly higher than his right when he speaks
and you shuffle closer,

because his light is of one you recognize,
of one you hope and yearn to fill your days with.

Take me back to where we loved,

when we loved,

and the world was good to us.

Come close,

let us put our bodies to good use.

Let us remind ourselves of the tenderness

we have gone so long without.

I only know how to live in love,

how to romanticize the struggle.

How to offer a hand and wipe tears away from cheeks,

how to compliment and lift another's spirit.

How to admire and acquire parts of others

I wish to strengthen within myself,

or build from scratch.

How to appreciate the kiss that meets me

after my feet have gone weak from a tiring day.

It's otherworldly, his selflessness and utmost adoration
for me and my jumbled ideas and ridiculous theories.

How he sits and waits and teaches me patience vicariously
because god, he knows how much I don't have it
and god — he loves me, anyway

and he continuously chooses to sit and wait and smile
as I sort through my restlessness. A nightly occurrence.

Heavy-eyed and spent
from conversation,
he softly asks me to come to bed.

Throughout centuries,
we have written of love,
bathed in it,
dreamt of starry nights
and lovely meetings.

It has always been there
and will always continue to be there.

As will pain and suffering,
as will hope and healing,
as will loss and growth.

How does one softly say,

"I don't know where my heart is,

but it's not with you."

But here they are and they love you

and it feels like you're dreaming.

You wake to a kiss and cry out of joy

because your heart is full for all the right reasons.

LOVERS IN THEORY

I couldn't even tell you what we spoke about
if you were to ask. Not because it wasn't of interest
but because I can't remember, because I was trying
to ease myself while maintaining his gaze, observing his hands,
thinking of where I wanted him to place them.

All of this was going on inside me
and it was merely his presence that put it there.

It's not often that we meet someone who makes us question
the particular chance of being:
this, now, here, and me — how this had to occur
and how that particular incident had to fall through,
in order for us to be sharing this small increment of time.

I couldn't even tell you what we spoke about
if you were to ask. Only that his subtle expressions of love
have kept me anchored for years.

A Study of Tenderness

I.   You see my heart for what it is
     and light up when you hear me rambling on about
     past-life theories, alternate dimensions,
     hypnotherapy — the possible history of you and me

     and it doesn't scare you
     and it's what made you come to love me
     in the first place.

II. And I cannot deny the opportunities
     that have revealed themselves to me
     once I opened myself up to love.

III. How I was completely myself
     and you offered your heart.

IV.   The softest intentions
        with your hand at my neck,
        leaving me
        more emotional and less intact.

V.   An arm that extends
        to embrace you at the cinema.

VI.   A hand that holds
        what the heart knows
        it must let go of.

VII.   Mouths that know desperation
        like, "the last kiss."

VIII.   A moment that asks for a lifetime,
        but receives minutes only.

I am no longer afraid of the distance,

this love will grow or it will flounder

but life will sort itself out.

LOVERS IN THEORY

There comes a time when love finds its end.

It dissipates, mourning the loss of its creation,

of what it took years to build.

There are many tears but no consolation.

We come to find this out on our own.

But it's over

and the world looks an awful lot like a graveyard.

One day, you look down

and you're carrying a shovel.

Ready to bury the feeling,

ready to live, again.

A heart that carries you through the devastation,

is a heart that knows the brutalities of life.

Both the raging gloom, the subtle peace,

what it truly means to stand by someone

in the thick of it.

To love someone enough to endure the uncertainty.

I could never find a proper explanation,
no logical reasoning for these feelings
I will soon be forced to forget
because how else does one move forward?

We can ask how the moon arrived,
host a debate about who put it there,
discuss how the sea became the thing
that could swallow us whole if we let it,
but with little to no resolve.

It is not a visible truth,
and yet I've reached a dreadful conclusion:

He is the love of my life,
but not in this life.

We've arrived at the improv
and I am seated across from a couple
that appear to be so madly in love
I practically ache with envy at their intimacy.

A cinematic vision,
dimmed lightening,
an audience to their story,
something that moves me.

To feel their romance at my corner,
while I am, evidently, falling out of it.

Our story was never one to be told,

but know that I remain loving you from here.

I spit you out like fresh blood, like habit,

not knowing when or where or how

I was wounded,

but as if I have always been this way.

Damaged yet relentless

and you are only just reminding me

of who I am

and the lengths I would go to for love.

By the time I arrive,

I find him on his knees.

I say, *look me in the eyes* — this is not a request.

But a taking,

a rapture,

an emotional slaughter.

The body

becoming both a place

of worship and ruin.

It was his choosing to move forward with this
and to my liking, something I wanted to explore.

He was in awe of me, often losing his composure
and slipping into a world he would never get out of.

I admit, I relished in the power.
I wouldn't take no for an answer,
but he enjoys this.

Look now, for I have only given him a taste
and he has since been kneeling at my feet.

I am absolutely drawn to films,

to journals and essays,

to poetry and photographs,

to any form of documentation

that yields to love

and provides proof of its history.

I. Kiss me where it hurts,

 soften the pain of the past.

II. A kiss is the work of magic,

 granting the fantasy of another life.

My heart holds your name

like it's the only thing it knows.

I spent years, years chasing a feeling.
A persistent feeling that hung over me
like there was something that needed to be
explored, attained, resolved.

But he clarifies, and after all the misleadings
you realize this isn't what you thought it was.

And his name has now come to mean more
than just a name — but a blaring siren,
a steady firing, a bullet to the chest.

He loved me then, half-past noon,
eating chicken lo mein and crab rangoons'
in the middle of his apartment.

We're reviewing the classics:

       pulp fiction, casablanca, the shining.

We've opened the curtains, asked meticulous questions,
revealed our secrets.

No greater love was ever built on anything less than honesty.

And you? he asks, "What is the first thing
you remember being afraid of?"
I reply, knowing at a relatively young age
that everything I love will one day be returned to the stars
and that in such insurmountable space,
I may never reunite with them, again.

This is why I've come to treasure every moment.
For this, too, now only lives in my memory.

Ah, the romantics.

Victim to the hour
thus we yearn to be timeless.

Not bound by the anticipation
of inevitable loss

when we are built on a love
that demands immortality.

An older gentleman at the book fair

takes a look at my poems,

tells me that they would name a street after me in Europe,

that it is the place for poets

where words attract the souls that need to hear them.

After briefly reviewing my work,

he asked me if I had my heart broken.

"Many times," I replied.

He releases a notable sigh,

heavy with times that have come and gone,

"forces us to grow, doesn't it?"

N.M.SANCHEZ

II.

The Meeting of Dreams

N.M.SANCHEZ

Could it be that our souls kissed

before our bodies touched

and that we have remained in conversation

throughout lifetimes we cannot remember?

What is this attachment to you?

This unbearable, one-sided attachment

to what is not — but what could be?

This fantasy I have created is certainly my own doing

and it consumes me:

A creation that invades its creator.

My heart is full of intense sentiments.

Love, full of love.

And you? Where do I start with you?

Or rather, when?

If love transcends time and space,

I wonder this:

When did we come face to face,

mouth to kiss, and how long has this sense

of belonging within me, belonged to you?

It is quiet in here, as it often is.

But every part of me is delighted,
awakened by the intensity of impulsivity,

the seconds of bravery I possess
between the love, the longing,

the tension of lovers
whose bodies have yet to meet.

I. I dreamt about you last night,

our souls must have been intimate elsewhere.

II. With a mouth like that,

I would give myself to him for centuries.

What do your thoughts of me matter

if you continue to hold her at the end of the day?

I am always *in theory*, partly a dream.

LOVERS IN THEORY

Late August, spent in the backyards of bars
with twinkle lights reminiscent of dreams.

I am adored in my silk dress,
admired for the waves in my hair
and the color of my personality.

I take a sip of your thoughts
and you drown in the corner of my eyes,
pure and crinkled with the softest of laughters.

How long will you continue to choose a memory
over flesh and bone?
She is here, she is waiting — and knowing this,
what will you do with it?

LOVERS IN THEORY

If there is anything I know about grief:
It's that it doesn't knock, but lets itself in.

It has made a home of me
and grief — it swims and sinks teeth
into my dreams, a mockery.

It bathes in a vision of love so pure,
in a love that knows nothing
but the shadow of its own potential.

In a love that will never see its beloved's face
but only sleeps with loss
and knows the purpose of tears.

How long before dreams

mirror barriers

and you realize

a reality without me won't suffice?

What if you took the leap?

What if you extended your hand to me?

What if we fell into a laughter

that would echo our love

for the next hundred years?

It's grown deep and absurd,

this ache, this longing,

the indisputable belief

that I was meant to love you.

Look at how unlikely our meeting was.

Look at the vastness of the universe

encompassing all the things we don't know

and the things we think we know.

Look at me, at us — together.

Here and now.

Isn't this some form of a miracle?

Are dreams not a glimpse into another life?

A doorway to another realm,

proof that we exist together elsewhere?

I must have loved you before — in another life,
beyond a dream, across centuries.

I wonder how many lifetimes you've had me like this.

How many sunrises you have awakened to,
how many we have experienced together.

How many times I have looked up at the moon
expressing similar sentiments.

There are worlds within this world

and one that solely belongs to you.

He takes me out for Italian,
the taste of romance — if there ever was any.

We're guided to a table by the water
and the breeze is as soothing as his voice.

A hand across the table that requests mine in return.

I ask the waiter for another minute,
I'm considering a future here.

Forget careful thought, I remain an impulsive lover
who knows what she wants.

I'll face the consequences later
but for now, "We'll start with the burrata."

It is possible that the lover you are

and the lover I've thought you to be

are two very different people

and the second does not exist.

I write to travel back in time,

to press my lips against the lining of a memory,

to touch a fragment that wishes to become

what it once was:

a thing to be felt and re-experienced — revived,

because to love you there

is better than to face the anguish here.

The way the body speaks its own language,

I'm closing in, exposed,

as open and as welcoming as a sunflower

in the middle of a summer heat.

All three things: lovely, vibrant, and youthful.

Am I close enough that the message is received?

He touches my face,

eyes to lips — *message delivered.*

Love and Psychoanalysis

She asks you to draw a door
and you think to yourself, "how silly, how child-like,"
you ask, "what for?" but she doesn't budge.

You grab the pencil, entertain her instruction
and unknowingly begin an illustration of the heart.

You have nearly finished when she asks you,
"what's behind it? if you could have anything,
see anything or anyone, who or what is there?"

And it brings you to tears,
this projection of love and longing,
of adoration and fantasy,
with each line you drew — an impending doom:

the distance between what could have been
and the reality of the choices you made.

Half the night, I'm yours
melting in your palm.

I have always wanted you this way
or bargained for you in that way
but find that this life will not let me have either.

That this love will never know peace
like the mere act of holding hands in the day time.

Not everything is meant to last
and not everything is meant
to be learned from — only endured.

Forgive me for praying that you'll call, again.

I want to spill it.

I want to tell you how often I think of you
but to say that *I dreamed of you* is far more acceptable,
an involuntary visit,
a light-hearted experience without intention,
secretly hoping you ache for the narrative.

I want to spill it, I want to tell you how often
I think of you.

No more songs with hidden meanings
I'm too afraid to convey,
no more dreams that speak to my feelings
without saying them directly.

I want to spill it.

I want to tell you how often I think of you,
I want to know if the feeling is mutual.

Dreams?

Why yes, let us speak of dreams.

Dreams as anchors,
dreams as memories from a past life,
a portal between worlds.

Dreams that reveal glimpses of secrets
from our past selves.

He teaches me about *soul recognition*, the possibility
that certain individuals once shared a history
surrounded by love, and that the identification of that other soul
could arise through intense, inexplicable emotion:

through dreams, in the slightest touch, in initial meetings
that elicit great feelings of familiarity.
          I have always been known to entertain this.

As if though there was a life I could not remember
but was only just returning to me now. In fragments.
Slowly, subtly — but with striking fervor.

He explains that not every soul we've experienced
in a previous life will recognize us now,
and that prompted an inner restlessness because
what if it were true?

What if you recognized a soulmate
but they did not recognize you back? And as a result,
that potential was lost? I'll admit, I am slightly afraid
because what if that's what's happened here?

You came to me in a dream

looking uneasy, uncertain, and worried.

A kind of mutual sadness filled the air

in a way that I cannot describe,

only in the way we looked at each other.

LOVERS IN THEORY

You were standing near the Ferris wheel,
picking at pink cotton candy
as the rides colorful lights reflected on your face

and I do this thing where I take a moment to myself
and assume the role of an outside observer — looking in,
as if from a window

and I imagine a world where we do not cross paths,
where I never come to learn of your existence.

It's a moment turned into a voluntary lesson,
a moment of which I fall sensitive to the intricacies of life,
its subtle work, the insurmountable possibilities,
both the mystery and miracle of knowing you.

You call out to me and I sigh in relief.
I am grateful all over, again.

A kiss in a dream — so vivid,

it is mistaken for a memory.

LOVERS IN THEORY

It's a torturous high, waking from a dream
and confusing it for reality, feeling as though
you were only remembering — something tangible,
something that once belonged to you
and was taken or lost or is waiting to be found, again.

But it's unexplainable, inaccessible,
and all that's left is this lingering feeling
of loss and disconnect.

An intimidating space

but an intimate one, nonetheless

where dreams offer the broken

an alternate ending:

both jolting and brief,

the worlds reveal themselves to me

and in each, it seems

as if I have always been full of grief.

Our story ends here
and it has been fulfilling.

I'll miss you, terribly
I leave you — lovingly.

Until the next life.

N.M.SANCHEZ

III.

A CONCEPT,
A PHILOSOPHY

What if, by nature, I am *insatiable*

and all that arrives will never suffice?

An observation:

perhaps you are as lost and confused as you are

because there are two souls within you

fighting to keep an appearance.

Who we present to the world,

who we are behind closed doors — it's exhausting.

I am living proof of my own paradoxical life,

the fluidity of personality,

the realignment of inner chemistry.

Maybe the soul contradicts itself often

because it's holding onto remnants

of who we used to be.

I found myself bargaining,

always bargaining

for more time, more love,

less distance and more intimacy:

to make his feelings known to me.

I.   I miss you. I loved you.

      We can never go back.

II.   I'm a fool for reminiscing.

      I'm a romantic and that's the tragedy.

Maybe it was love,

maybe you knew before I did.

That unexpected surge of energy,

      the bliss,

the unexplainable feeling

that something wonderful is coming.

Sometimes you pour your heart out
and nothing comes back.

Sometimes you pour your heart out
and the world falls onto your lap.

Keep trying.

The choice is up to you:

kiss me now or only dream of it later.

I'm just trying to put my heart in the right place this time.

In tender hands — with people who love me, too.

Look at all the ways we have so gravely attempted guidance:
What does astrology say, or the psychic?

How many of us turn to these outlets
as a means of understanding ourselves better?
As a means of understanding the world around us?
Lost in our own complexity — seeking answers.

I've come across his name four times today
and my oldest friend tells me
that this is the universe's way of speaking to me.

I entertain her for a moment.
But deep down I know I've exhausted all solutions
to the point of embarrassment.
I've explained myself.
I've listened, I've *been* listening.
But him and I are no longer tuned to the same frequency.

The worst thing to a person

who realistically knows that a certain situation

will lead to a standstill,

is the hope that lingers and tells you that it isn't,

the hope that sweet talks you into thinking

you might be the exception.

I long for a sort of tenderness,

an alluring romance,

to be touched with such pure intentions

I turn to gold.

I am tied to things,

       to people,

            and places

that never asked to hold the rope.

I am learning to love myself, again
and it is absolutely liberating.

There are moments of uncertainty,
instances where hope is as out of reach as the next ten years,
and dreams fall short of anything tangible.

But I'm trying to embody the mantra
where everything is possible,
where the world is ready and waiting
and has even pulled out a seat for me.

What a woman to admire,
what a woman.

Imagine how I'll love when healed.

What I deserve and what you are willing to give

are two very different things:

I've learned that this is not the place for me.

I yearn for an inner peace,

a tender purpose,

to give and feel fulfilled in return.

The distance between how I feel

and what I know I have the potential to feel

is devastating.

It's an ongoing process,

but when you come to love yourself more

than the need for validation,

you will know freedom.

There is some sort of creative power
that underlies a broken heart.

To be in love is to be moved
beyond measure,
but there is a stronger force at work
when one has crumbled to their most vulnerable parts
and the mind quickly does what it can to heal the body.

Because sadness invades, it swarms like a virus
the body is desperate to rid itself of
through a variety of mediums: such as art,
within the healing properties of music, in travel.

And what I have witnessed repeatedly
is that a broken heart could make a poet out of anyone.

I have written texts that have brought me to tears

over lovers I would never see, again.

And it is not so much a matter of wanting them back

      or trying to retrieve our time together,

but a matter of my own nature

and its tendency to tune into the permanence of endings,

the tendency to stress my own mortality.

LOVERS IN THEORY

I assume that, ultimately, the proper use of my time
and heart's ticking is seeking and obtaining
a sense of security, a warming soundness
as I sleep next to a love who has shared my deepest secrets,
desires, and cries — a co-authored history.
A bond which has evolved from senseless passion
to compassion, to a mutual understanding
with a kiss of respect.

      My trouble is my tendency to romanticize,
to seek the excitement, to reach a high that is otherwise lost
to a realist who accepts the burn-out, a diminished wanting.
I cannot bring myself to know it and by it
I mean defeat, the loss of intimacy, the loss of exhilaration
and so I chase the burning flames
and the butterflies at the pit of my stomach

      because a romantic is anything but a realist,
a romantic runs to the object of desire,
to anything that reminds them
that they have a heart and that it beats to feel.

The more natural the connection,

the more devastating the disconnect.

Interviewing Intimacy

A hand that comes to discover the body,

a connection that forms between your thoughts

and crevices — the spell of your thighs

a bond, an appreciation for the extravagance of you.

To love oneself

is to conquer all that exists outside of it.

To embrace the sensual aspects of my nature
is to accept the very things that make us human,
an act so pure and necessary.

To be touched and noticed,
to be heard and appreciated,
to be made to feel alive.

LOVERS IN THEORY

It was time I began to admire my own heavenly features:

the widening of my hips,
the boldness of my thighs,
the *salsa* in my steps
with a mouth sweet like *mamey*.

I carry a delicate presence, skin like café con leche
with hair and eyes the color of Cuba's precious cafecito.

— An east Havana dream
with a heart like that of my mother's.

Love has made me selfless,

illusions of love made me selfish.

Seventh session at *Amelia's* restaurant with a young bartender full
of questions and no one to turn to.

A warm affinity is established over drinks
and dear conversation.
He delves into the disruption behind his green eyes,
laying out his own personal torments.
"How do you do it?" he asks,
"How do you know if they're the one?" he presses,

"She doesn't want more for herself — she's complacent
and I'm torn between waiting her out
or finding someone who could naturally match my energy."

We couldn't be friends 'cause god knows

we were meant to be lovers,

doomed to never belong to each other.

LOVERS IN THEORY

I asked myself, what would it take to be happy?
To surrender myself to the one who loves me so effortlessly?

What lies at the base of my troubles,
of my inability to remain still?

And I've come to the conclusion
that in order to obtain any sort of peace,

in order to remain present and appreciative:
I need to relieve myself of all the fantasies I'll never live.

Love me hard

or leave me — quickly.

I feel as though everything

I have ever fought for

has tricked me into thinking

it wanted me back.

I knew it was from the heart,

because I cried as I wrote it.

A Vulnerable Proposition

What is more beautiful than to be understood
in a world that cowers at the unfamiliar?
In a world that does not know
where to place you?

Your touch exudes understanding,
a gripping energy,
I know a tender love when I see one
and I am ready to be devoured.

A Conscious Breach

You've reached so far into me

that trying to return to myself

has become more of a task

of trying to rid myself of you.

All of these extraordinary people,
splendid personalities that walk about
and the magical complexity of it all,
of life, of meetings, *purposeful or accidental*

but how would we know the difference?

And to think of those
that I have been lucky enough to know
is to also think of those I could have loved,
if only I had known them.

A blessing in disguise,

thank goodness

you didn't love me back.

Listen — just listen,
the hardest part of anything
is getting started.

So take the plunge.

Remember that it is always the right time
to let go of anything that feels wrong.

It didn't happen the way you wanted,
but it happened the way you needed.

You'll see.

Two lovers, could you imagine that?

One for life

and one for the art of it all.

Notably frowned upon,

innately exhilarating,

the landscape of an artist's imagination.

Just ask Picasso, ask Giacometti,

ask Rodin and Frida

about the marriage and their muses.

I want to protect everyone. All the time.

The way we can be out here, loving others

who don't even care to check in on us.

I wish I could protect people from that somehow,

from the reality of not being wanted,

from the misery of not being loved back.

Real connections are so pure, so few and far in between,
not something to be fabricated but people sure love to try.
    And it's nothing against them.

We're all just trying to feel something:
to be seen, heard, and experienced.

A thing to be observed, touched, and detected,
chosen amongst the crowd.
    Different enough to be thought of.

It's only natural.
Sometimes we've even convinced ourselves
that it's happened, when it hasn't.

We formulate ideas, perceive our own projections
as an objective reality when their "love"
is merely our own staring back at us.

This is why rejection hits us two-fold,
unrequited love like ricochet.

I've stopped internalizing their behavior towards me
and justifying their actions as something I deserved.

But that's always been the art of manipulation,

being convinced you've always been the problem
and that you had it coming.

What I wanted was acknowledgement,
a verified truth, a steady "yes."

Love felt alone is not nearly as satisfying
as love made together.

And in my own seclusion, I faced suspicion.
I had to ask myself if it even happened.

Everyone's a drink away from missing
an ex love, a past life, a lost opportunity.

I. I held the hands of time,

flirted with reality

and became my own dream.

II. I've been my greatest romance,

the rest is simply incentive.

ABOUT THE AUTHOR

N.M.Sanchez is a Cuban-American author based in
Miami, Florida. *Lovers in Theory* is her second collection
of quotes, prose, and poetry.

Note to readers:

Thank you all for your continuous support and encouragement.
With absolute love and gratitude, N.M.Sanchez

Instagram: @n.m.sanchez

Printed in Great Britain
by Amazon